Floral Design

COLOR BY NUMBER COLORING BOOK

Jessica Mazurkiewicz

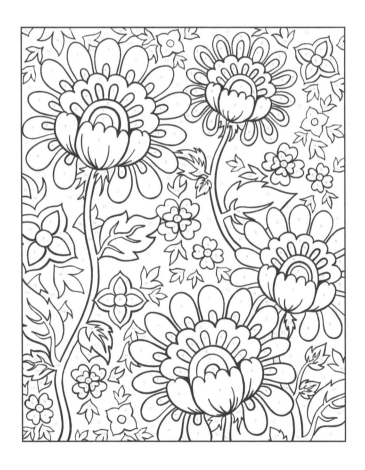

Dover Publications, Inc.
Mineola, New York

Bibliographical Note

Floral Design Color by Number Coloring Book is a new work,
first published by Dover Publications, Inc., in 2014.

International Standard Book Number

ISBN-13: 978-0-486-79385-6
ISBN-10: 0-486-79385-0

Manufactured in the United States by LSC Communications
79385018   2019
www.doverpublications.com

This coloring collection features forty-six full-page floral designs for you to color. Each plate is shown in full-color on the inside covers. You can duplicate these images simply by following the color guide found on the inside front cover, or choose your own colors for a more personal touch. As part of Dover's *Creative Haven* series for the experienced colorist, each plate is highly detailed, and enclosed in a border for a finished look. Plus, perforated, unbacked pages offer you the opportunity to experiment with any media you like, and make displaying your work easy!

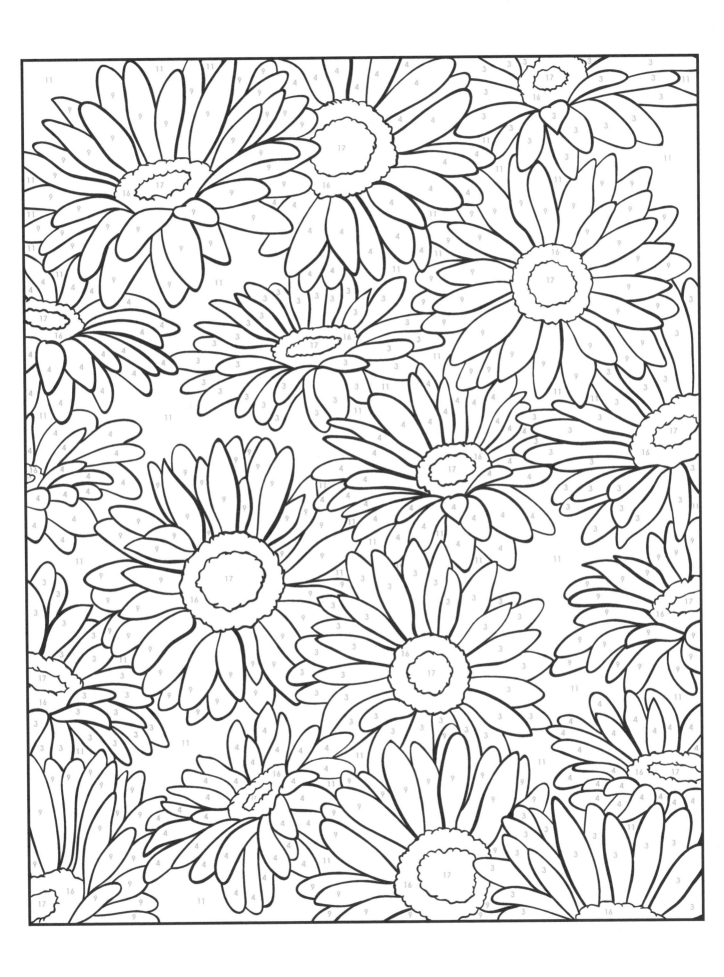

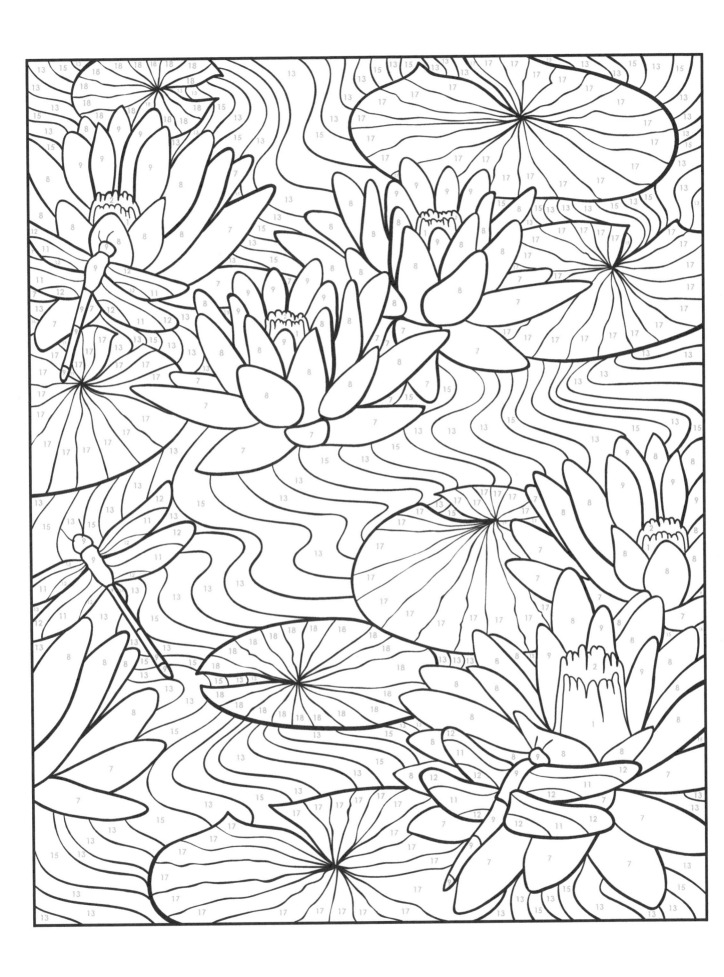

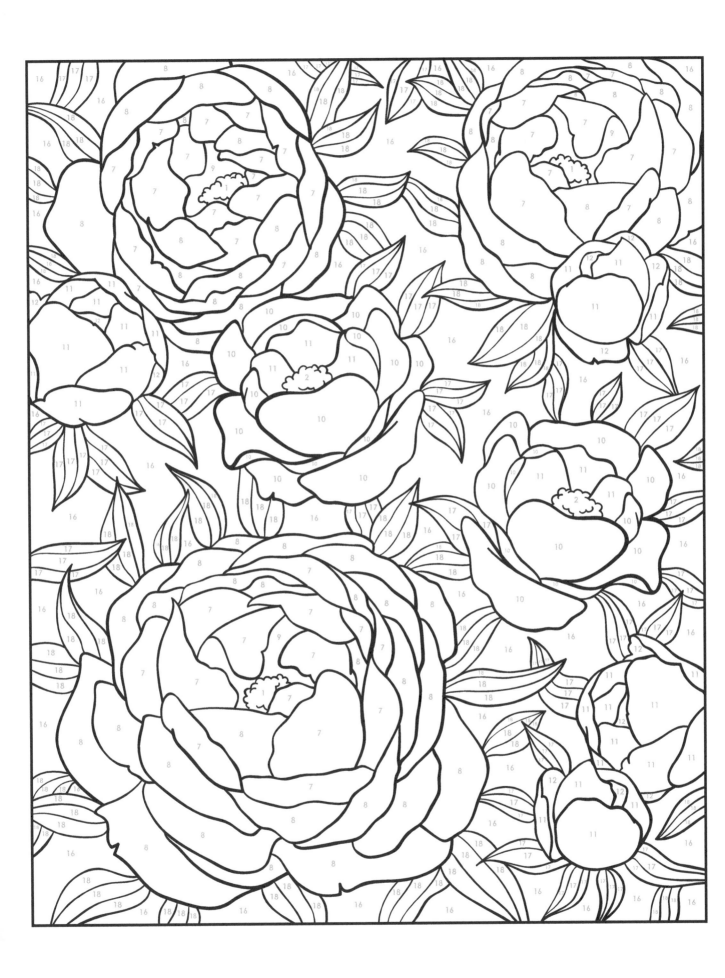

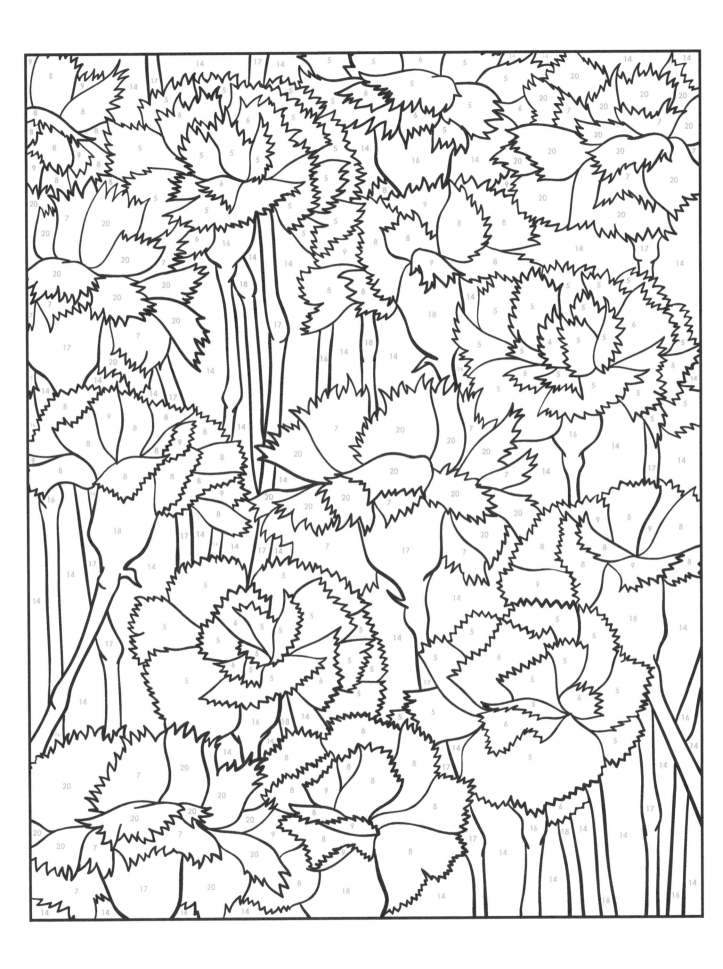

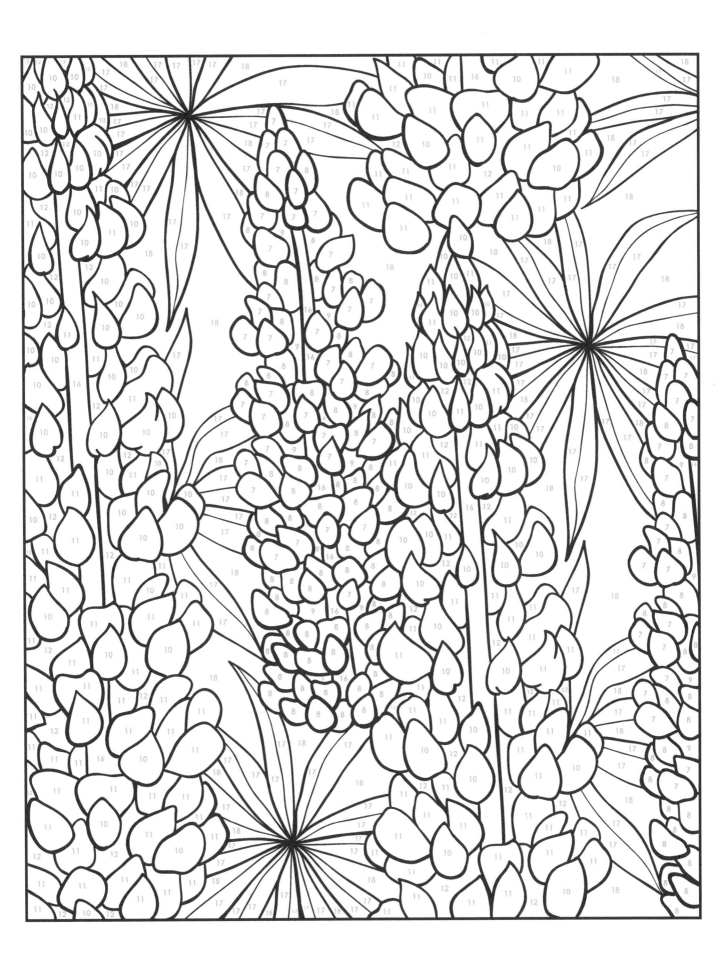

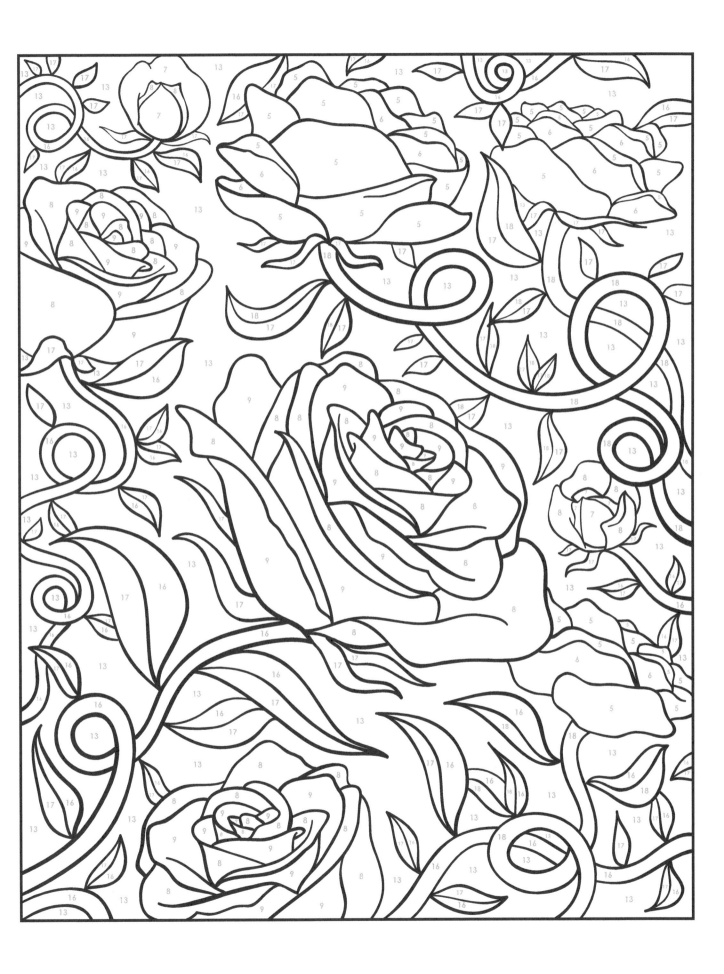

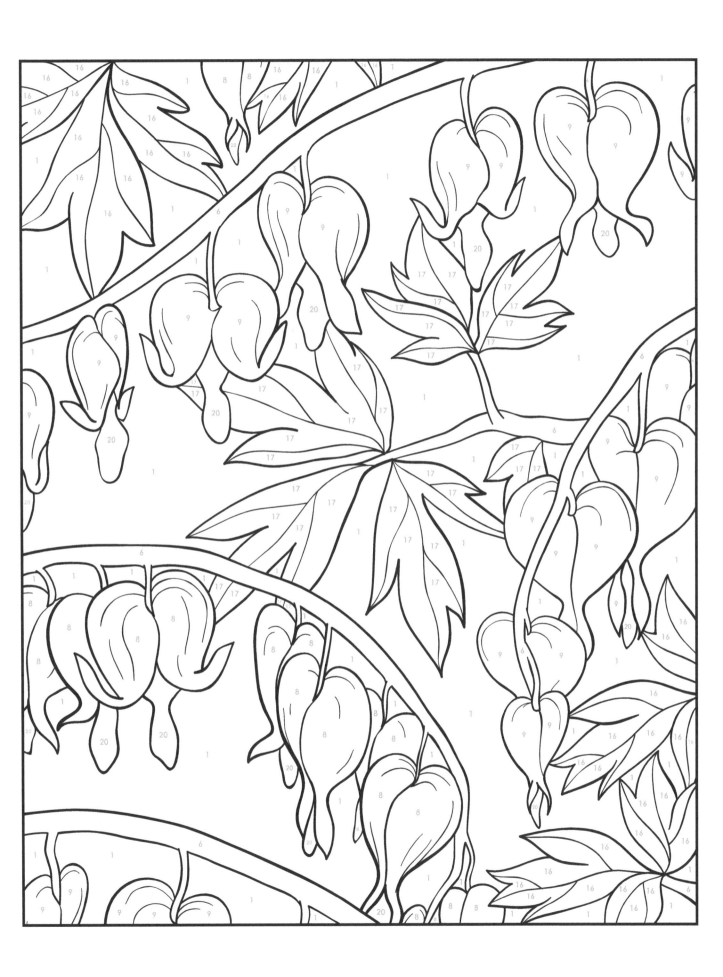

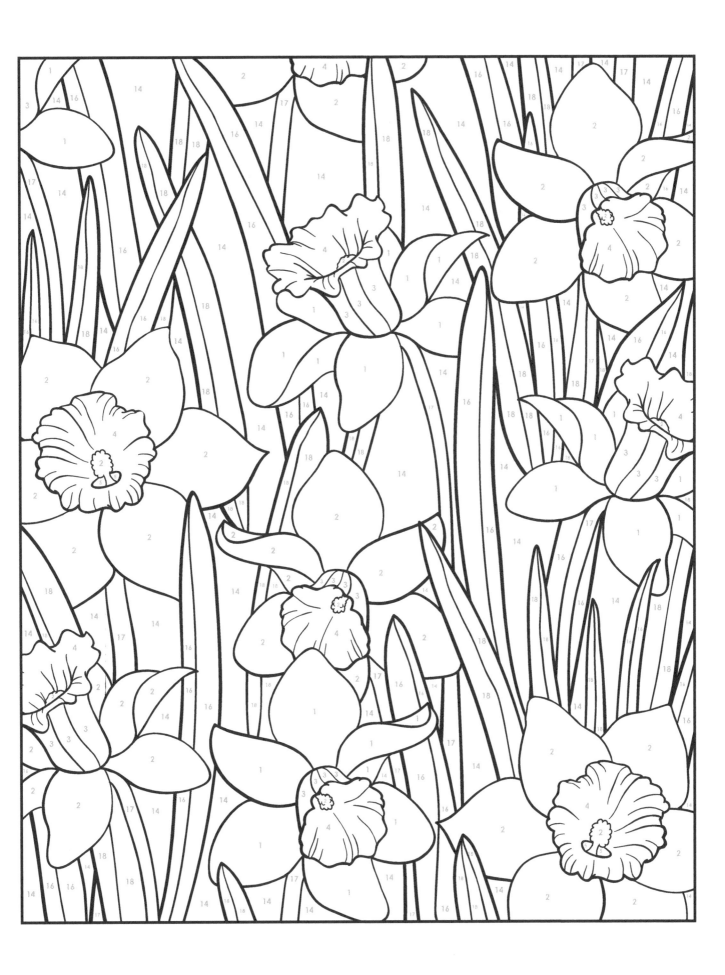

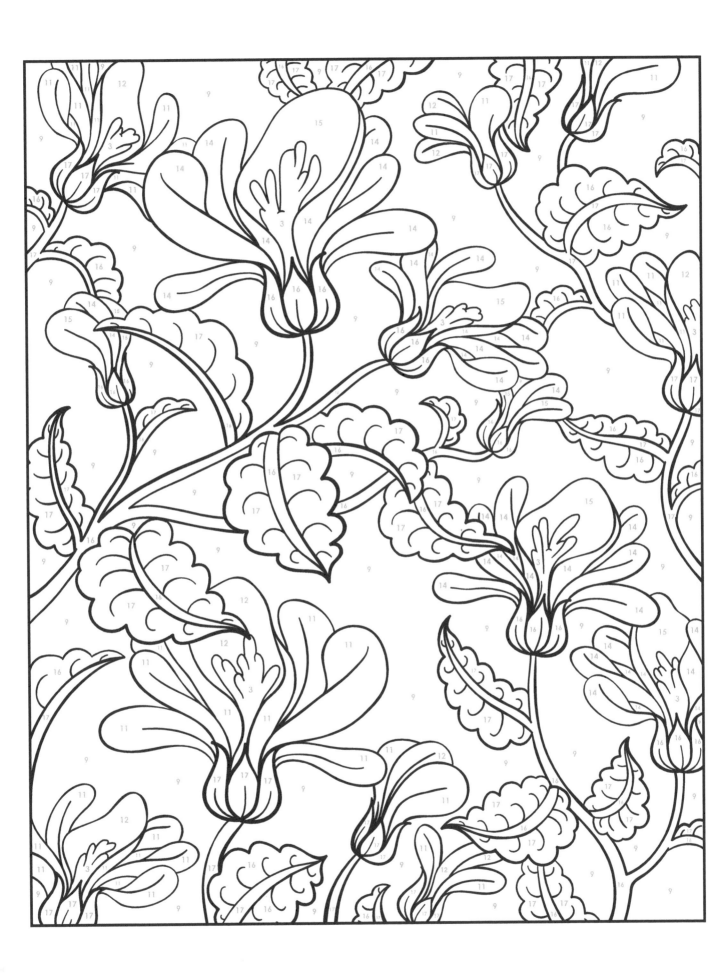

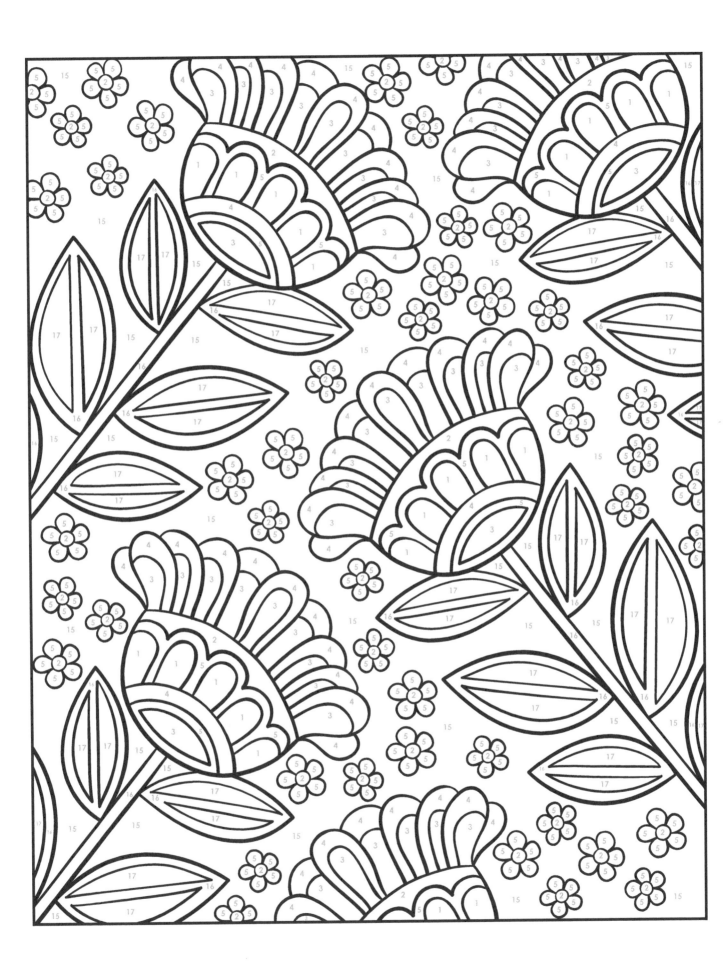

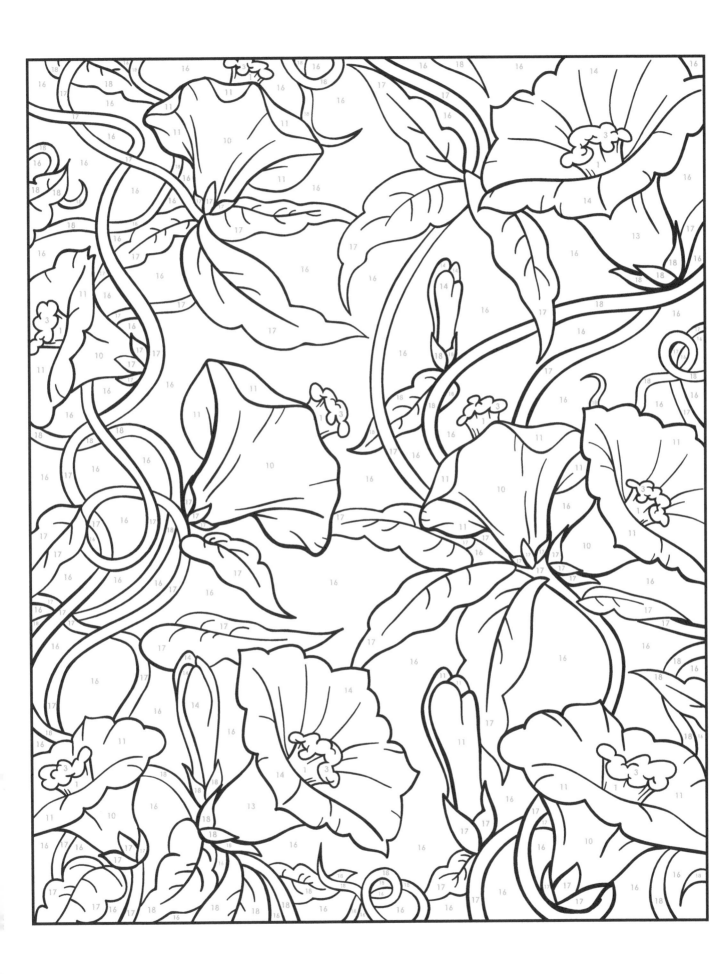

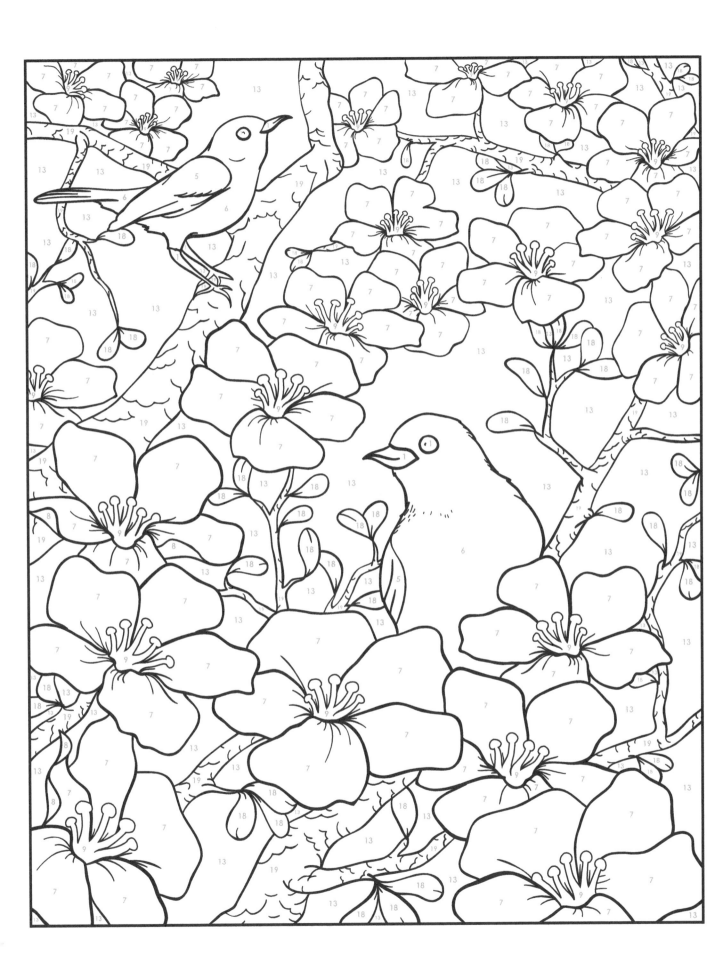

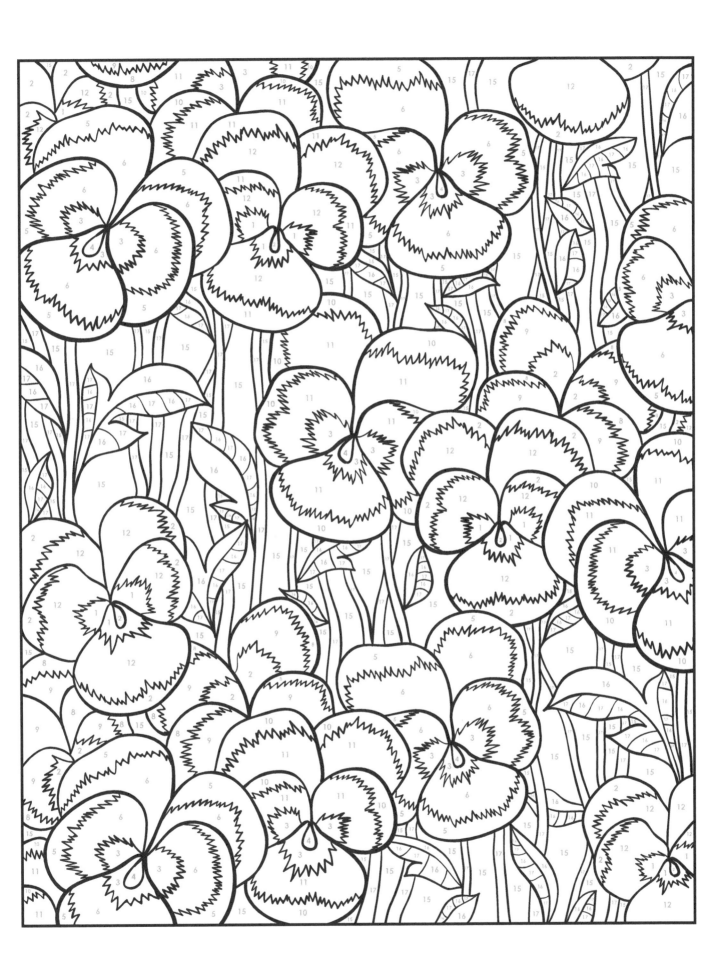

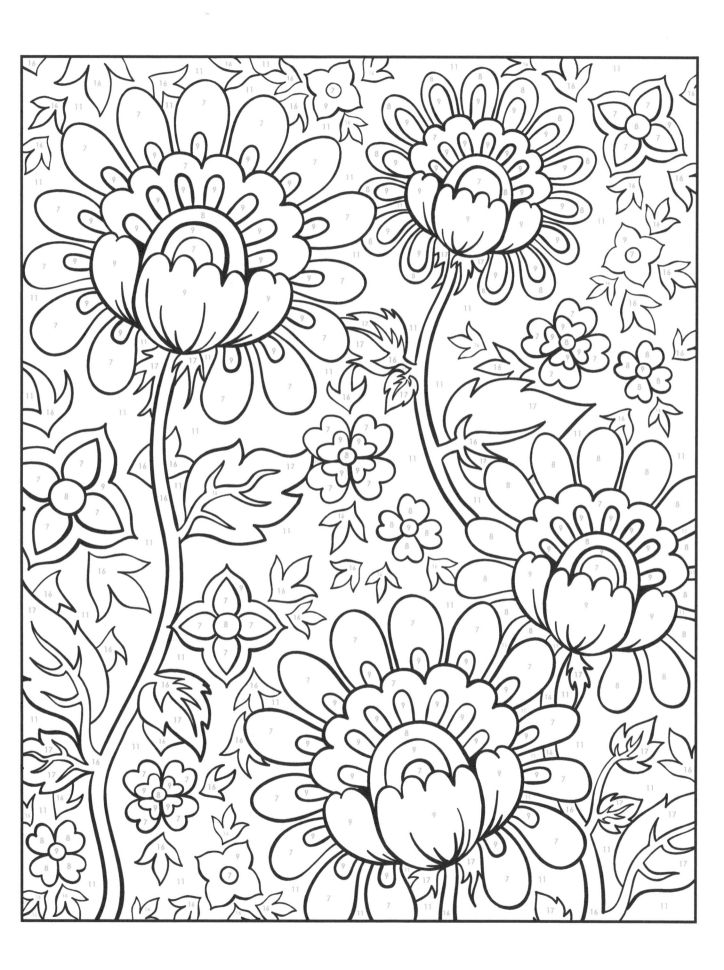

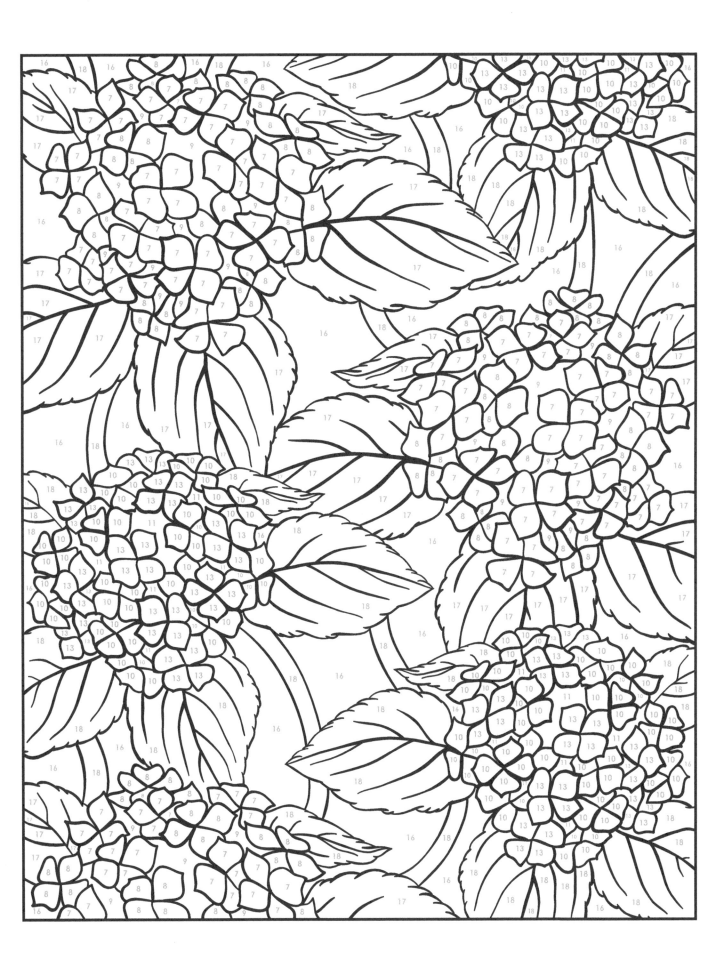

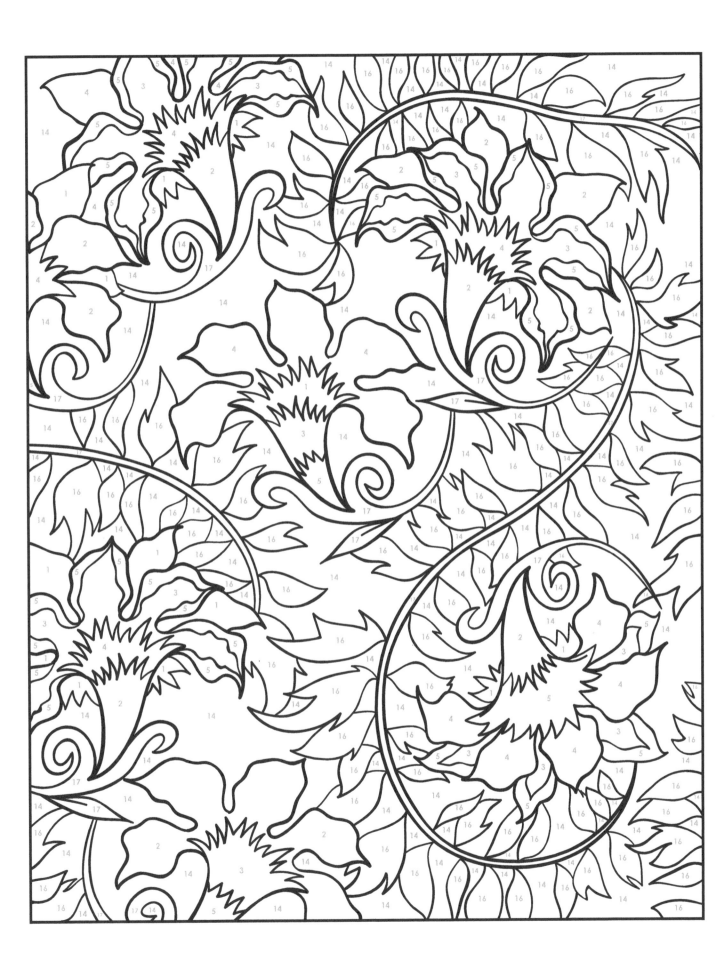

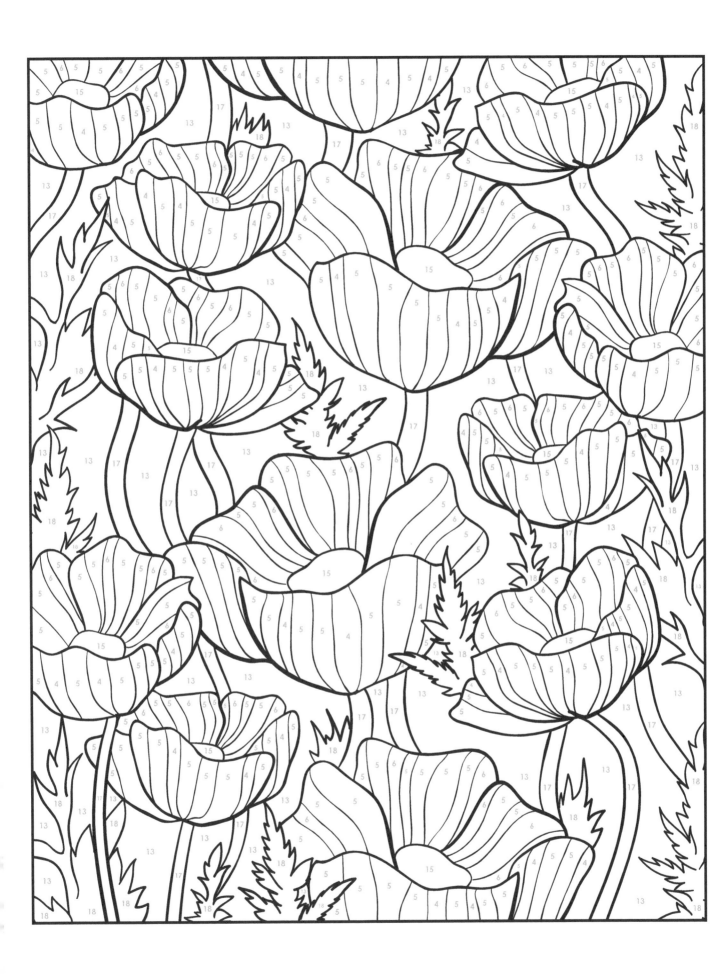

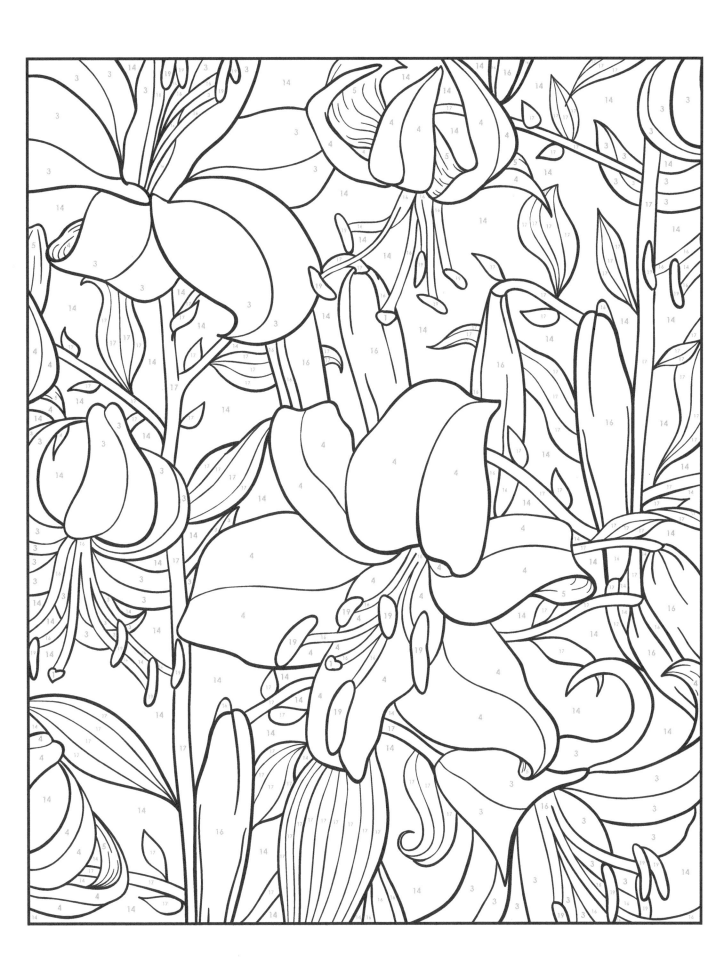

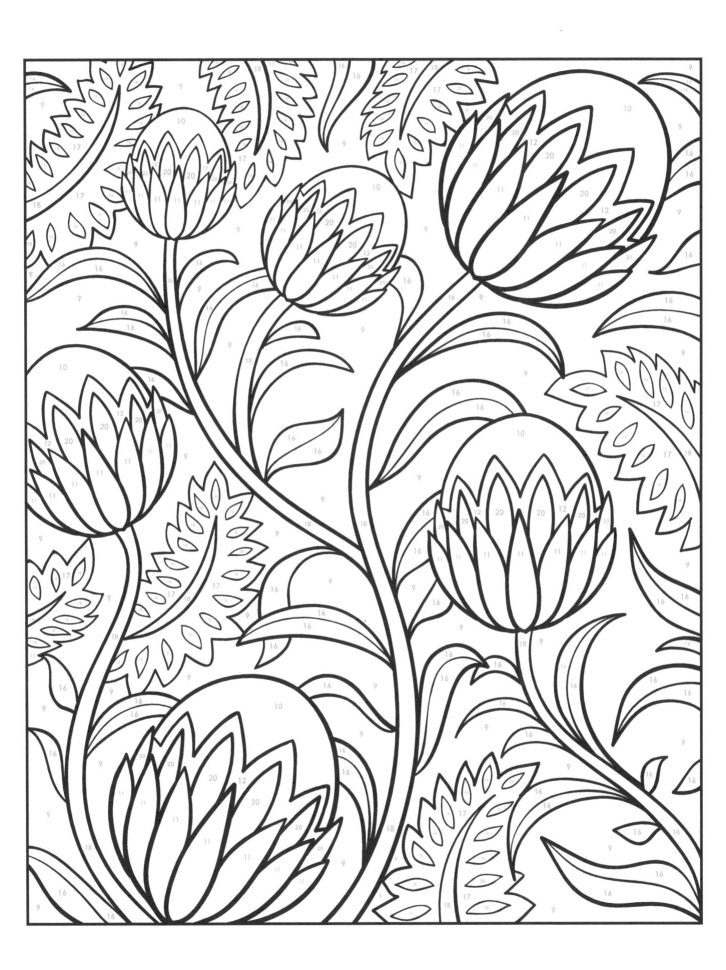

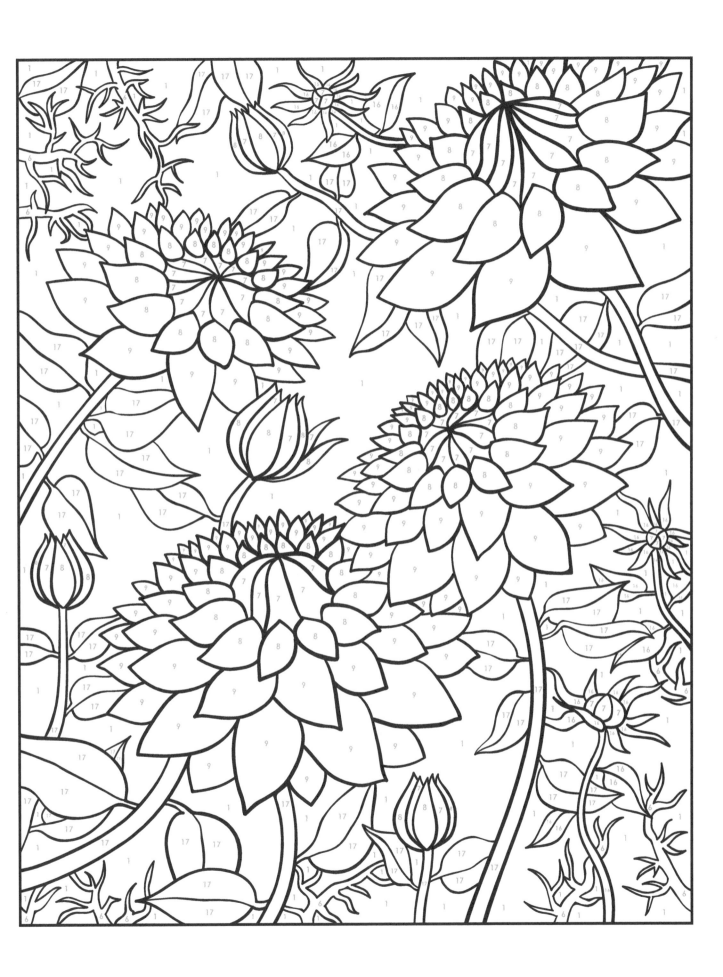

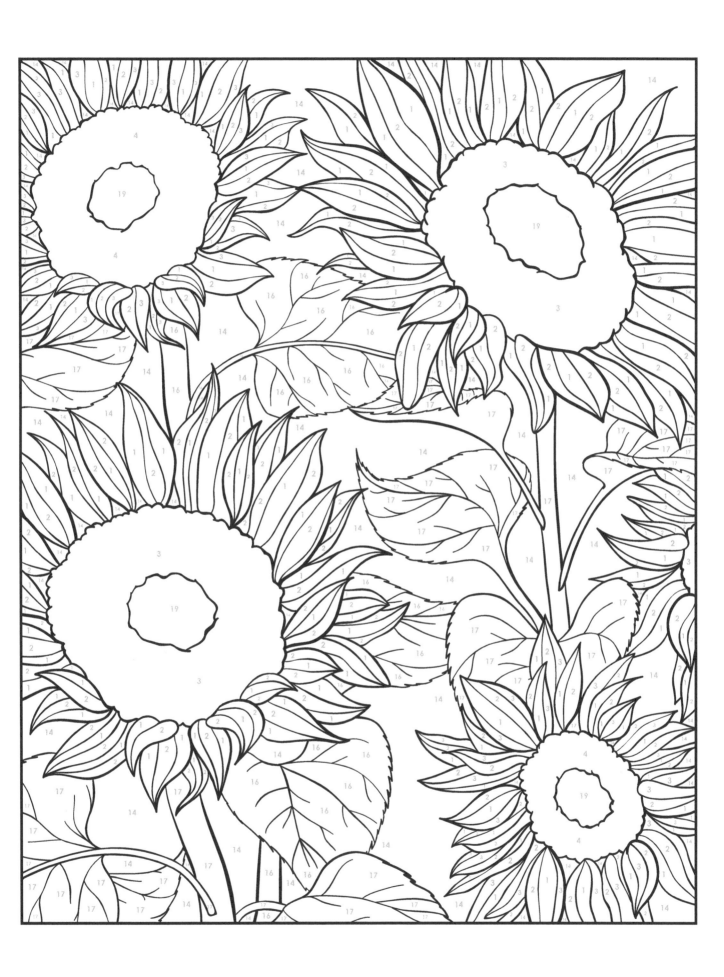

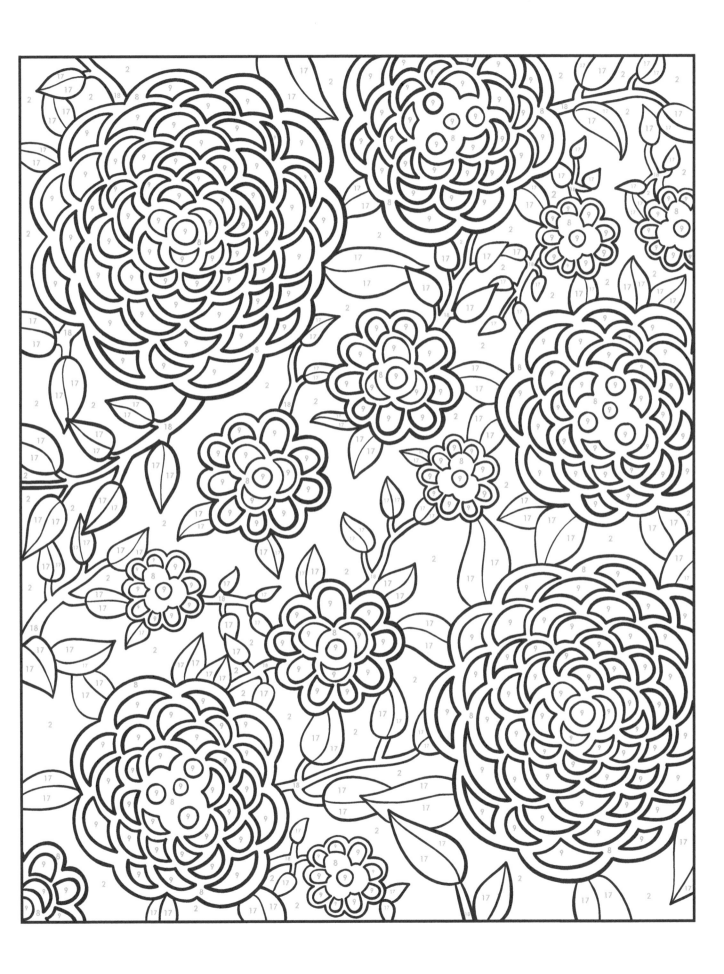

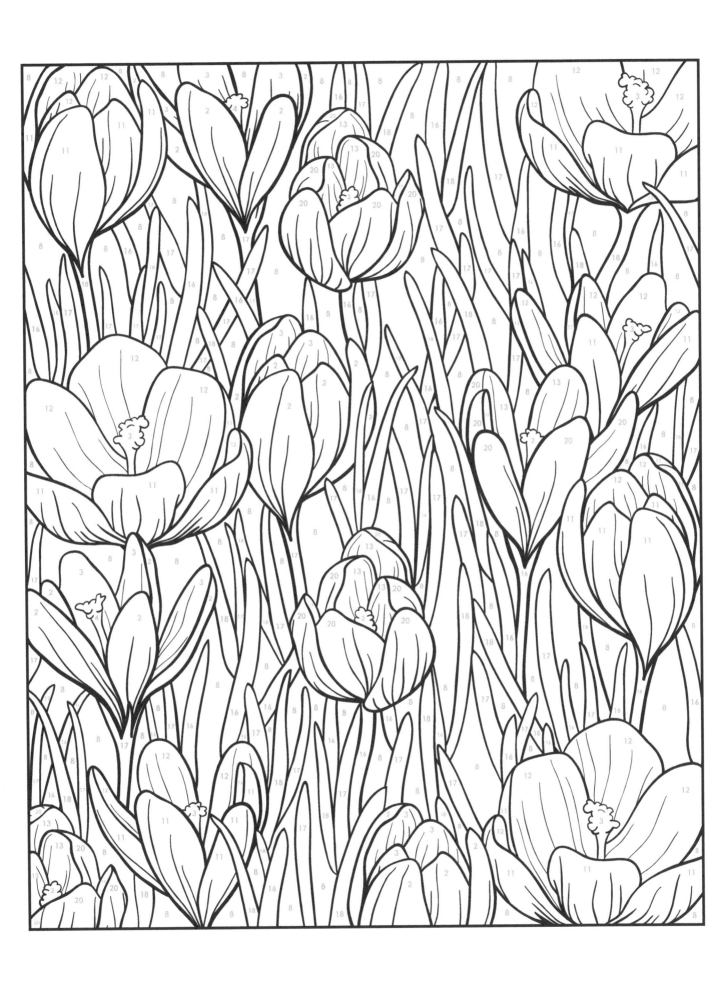

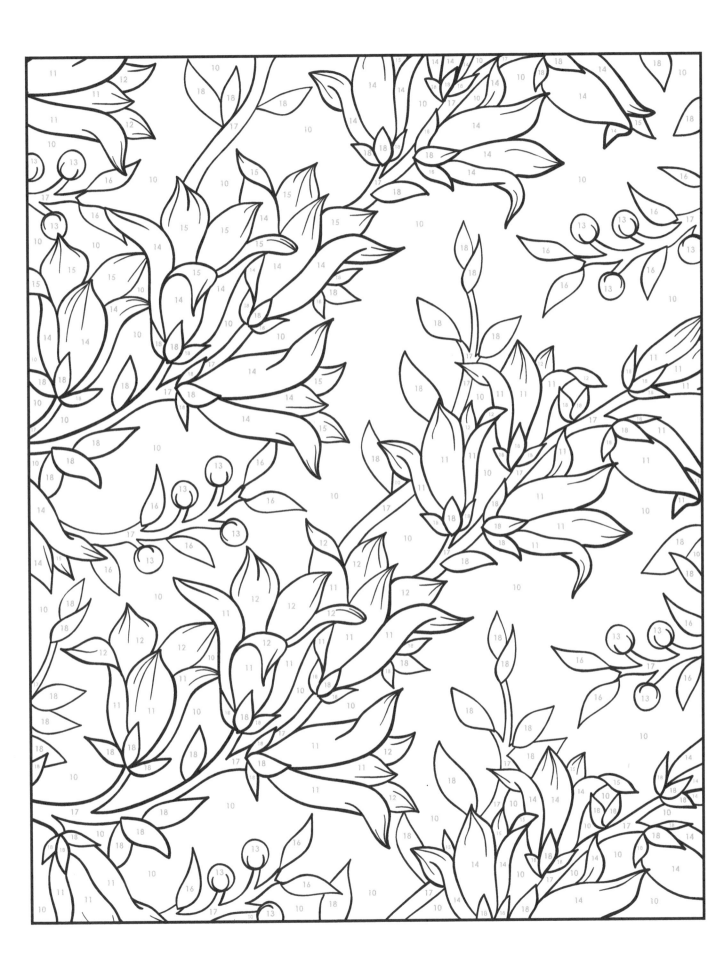

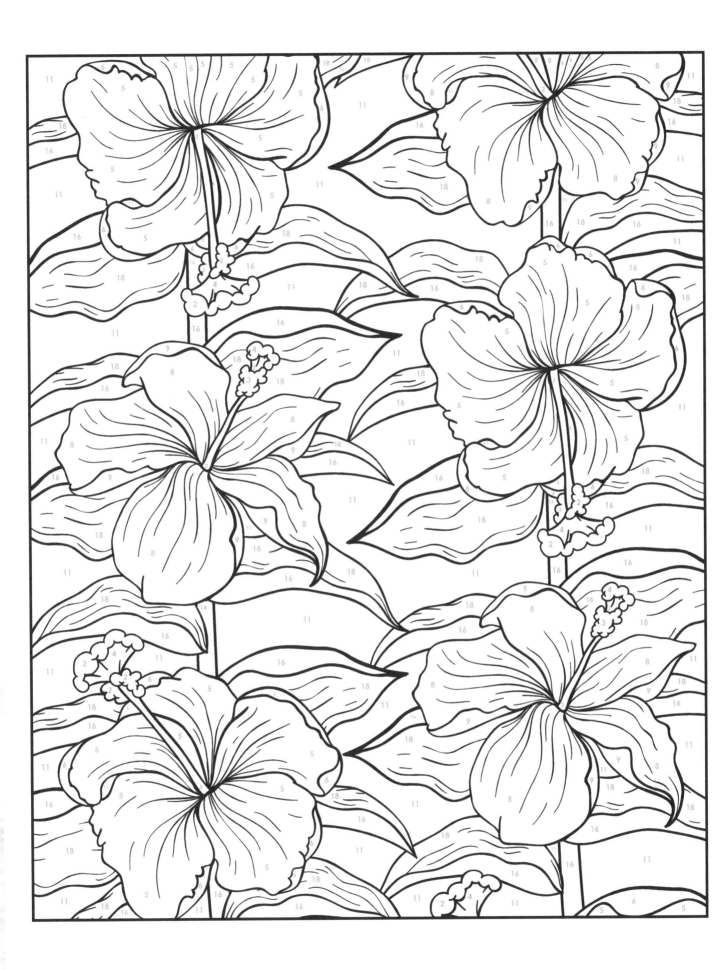

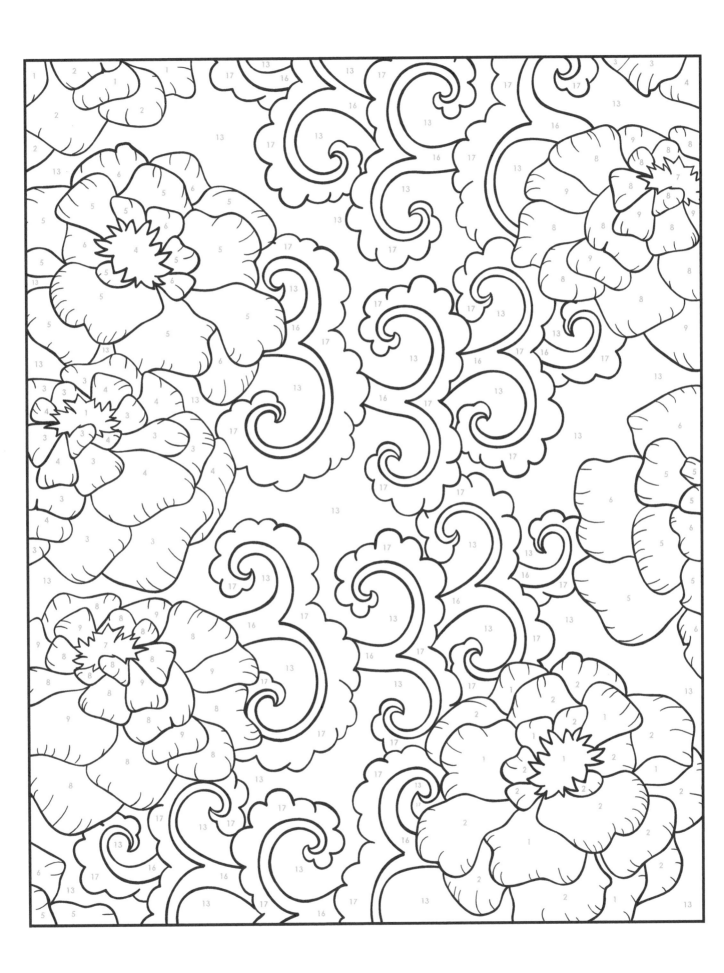

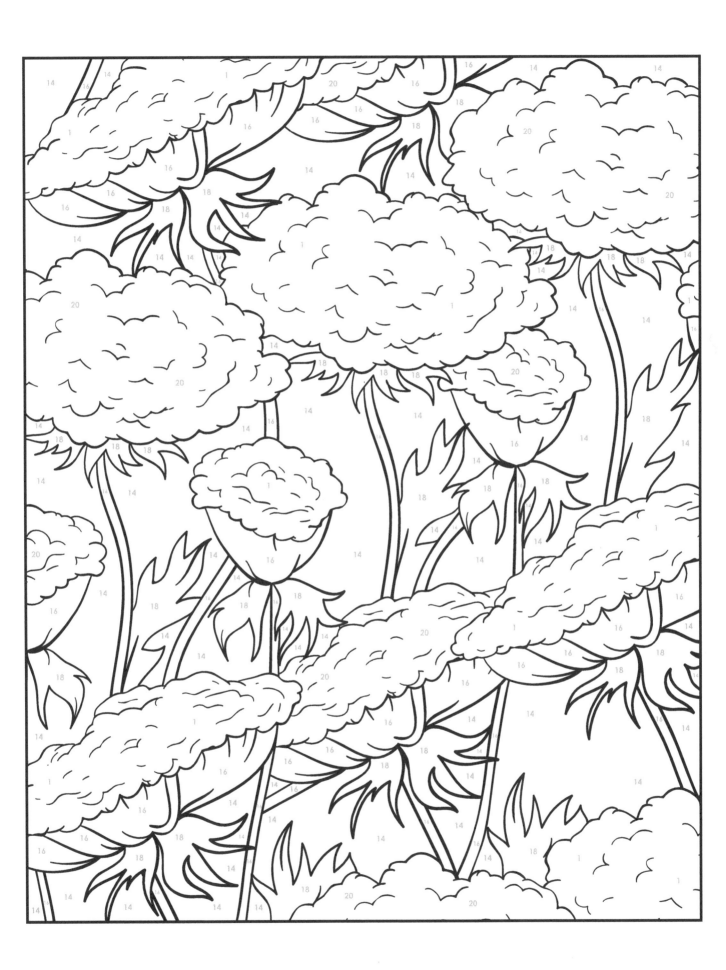

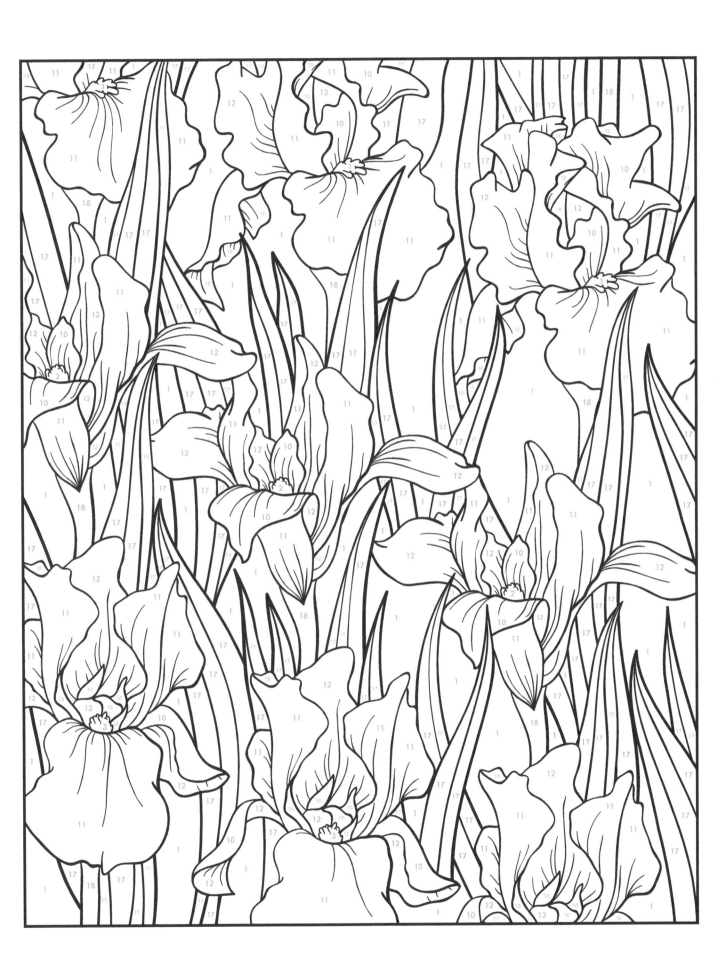

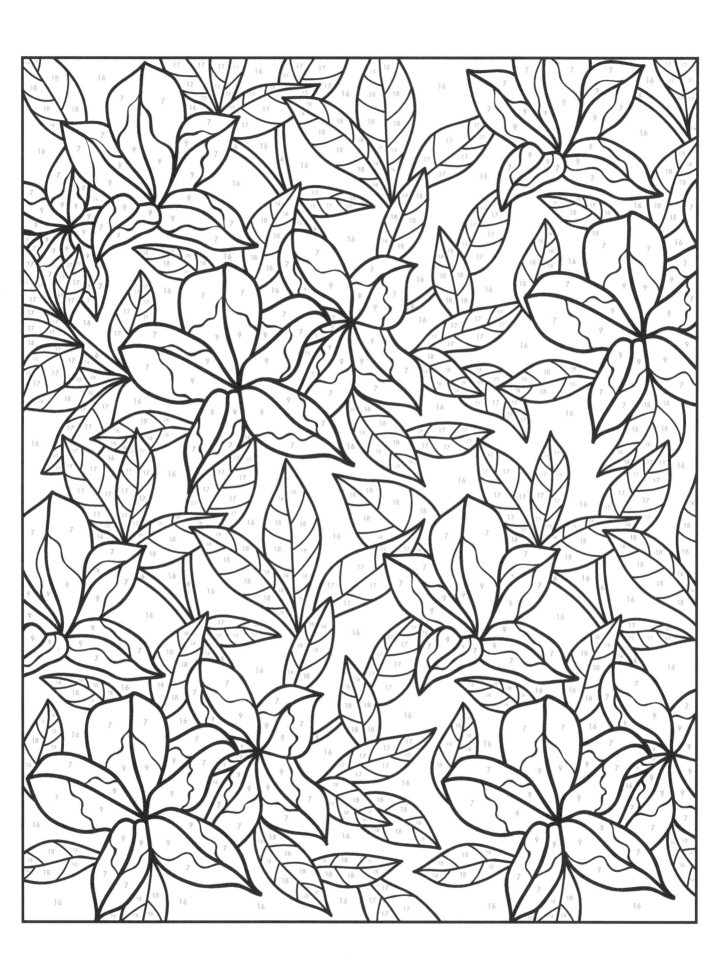

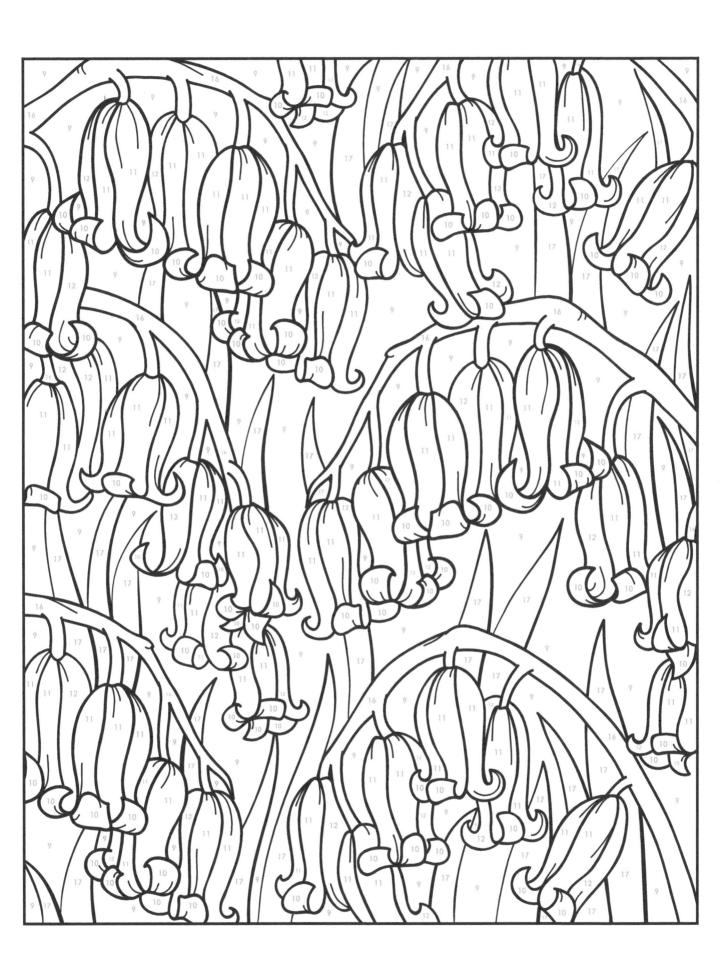

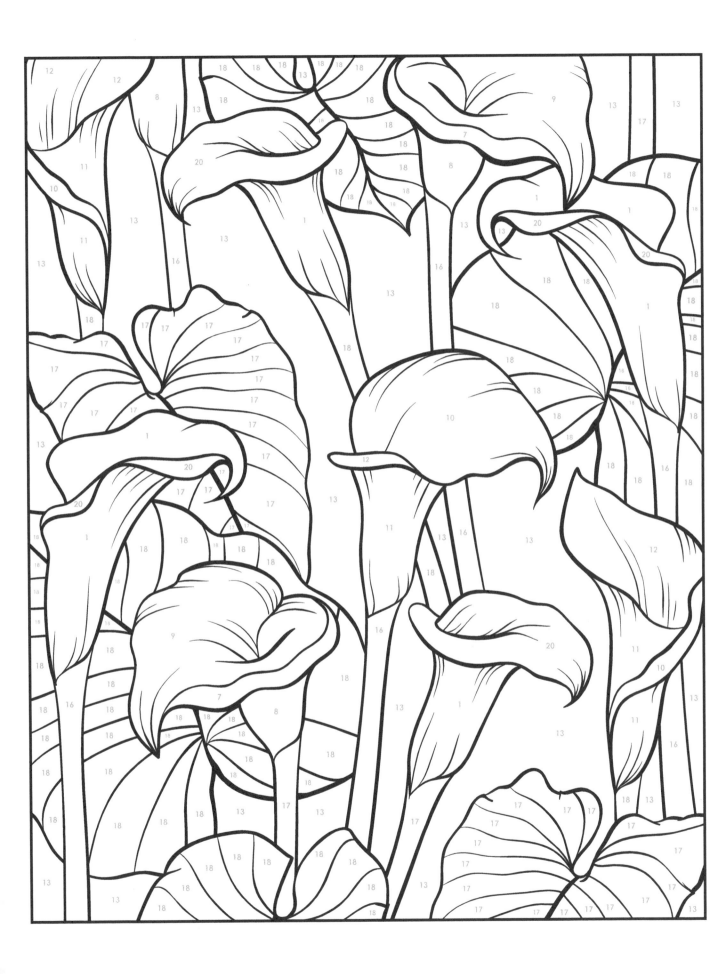

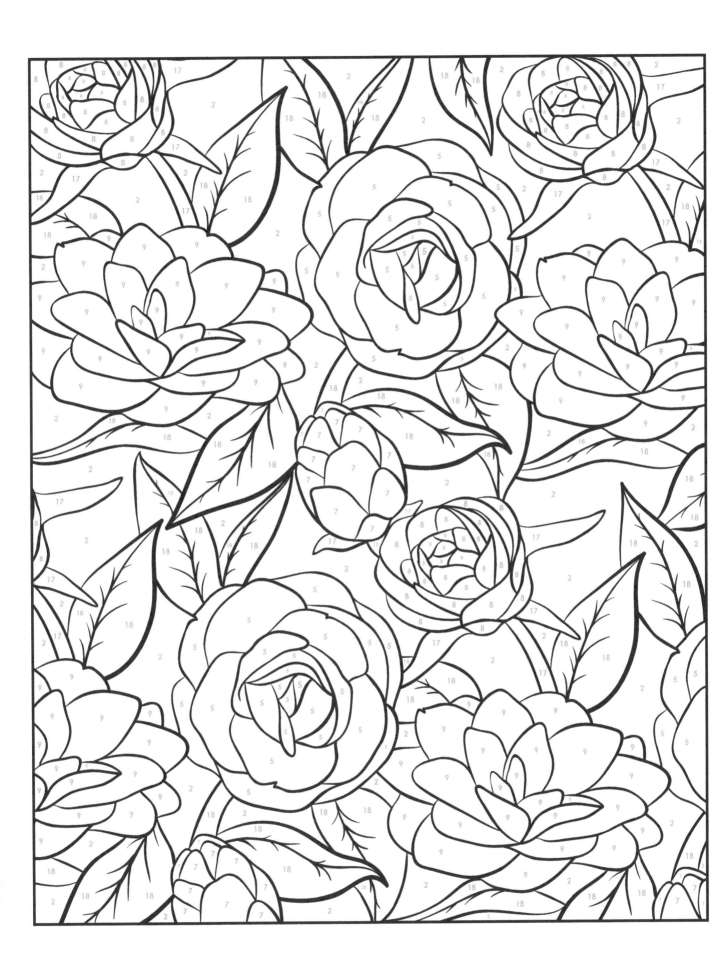

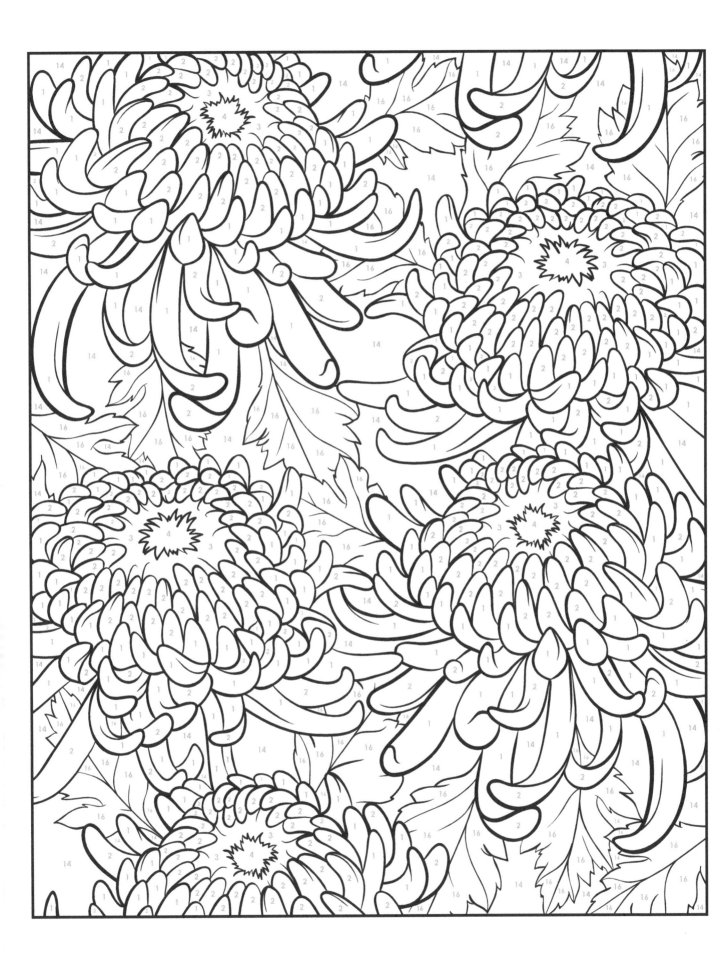

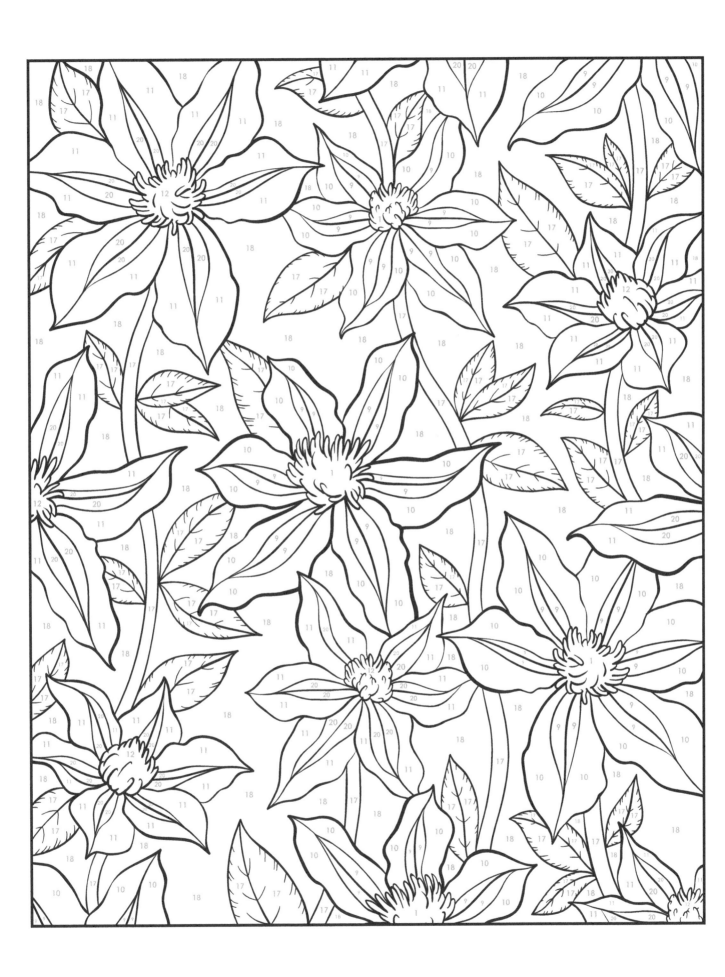

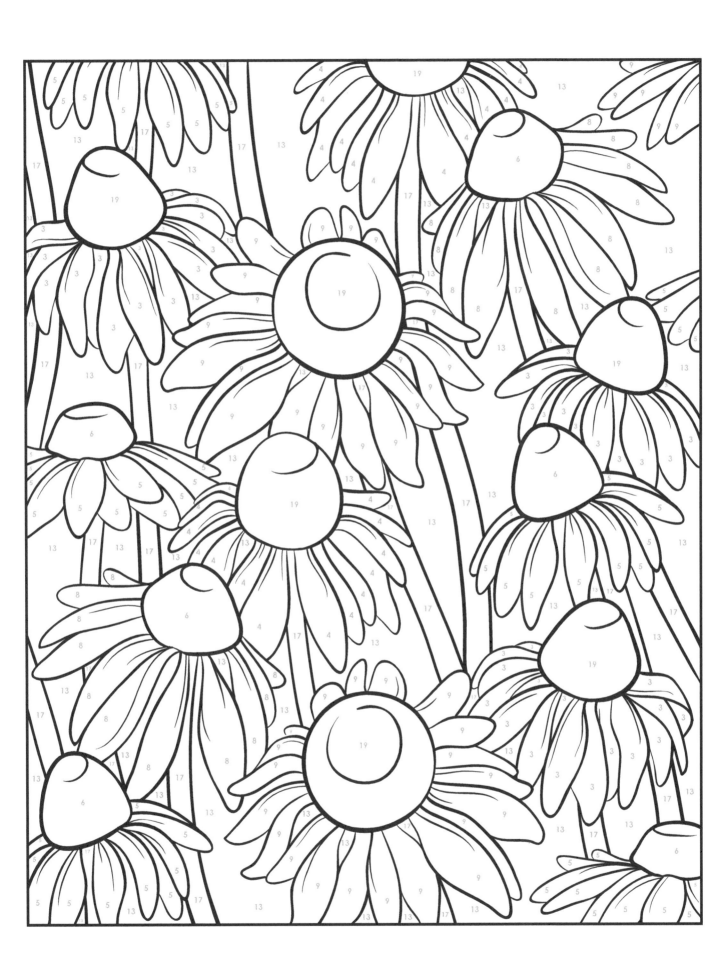

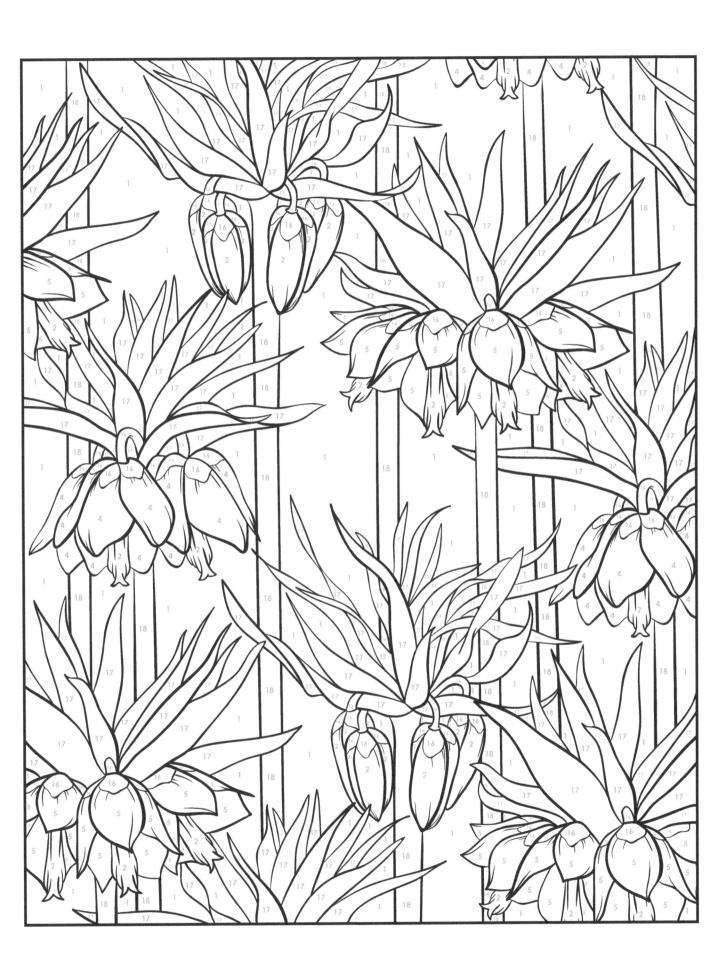

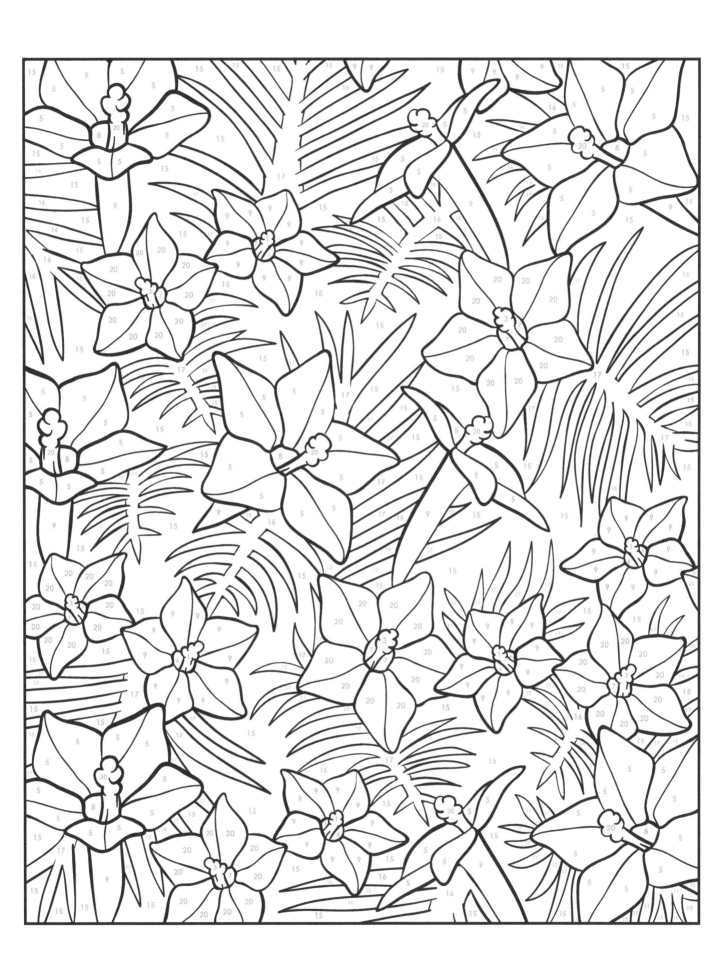

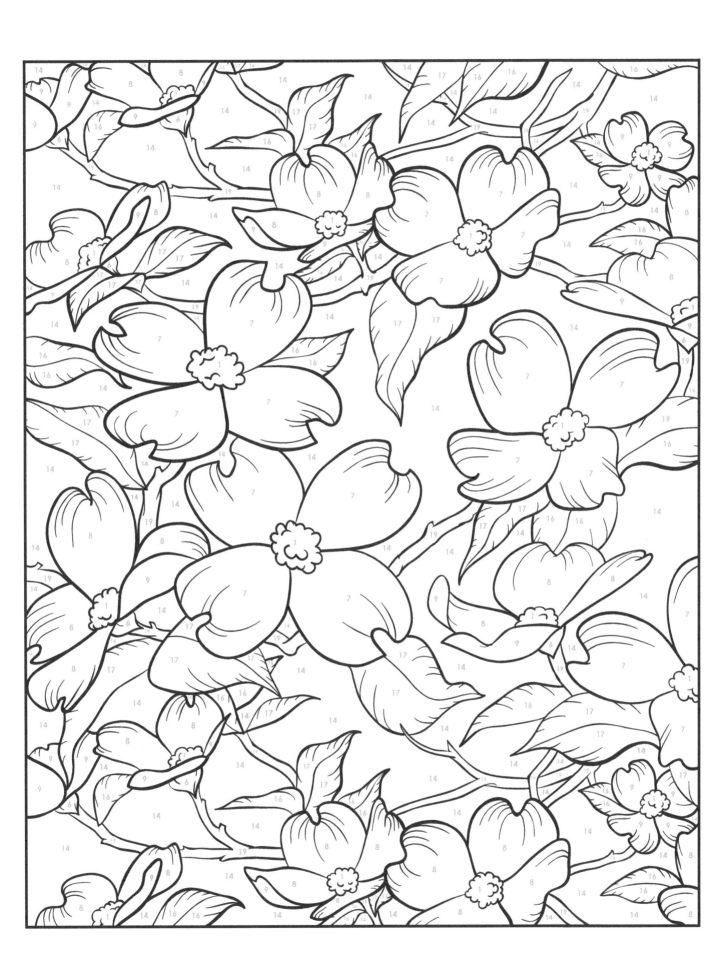

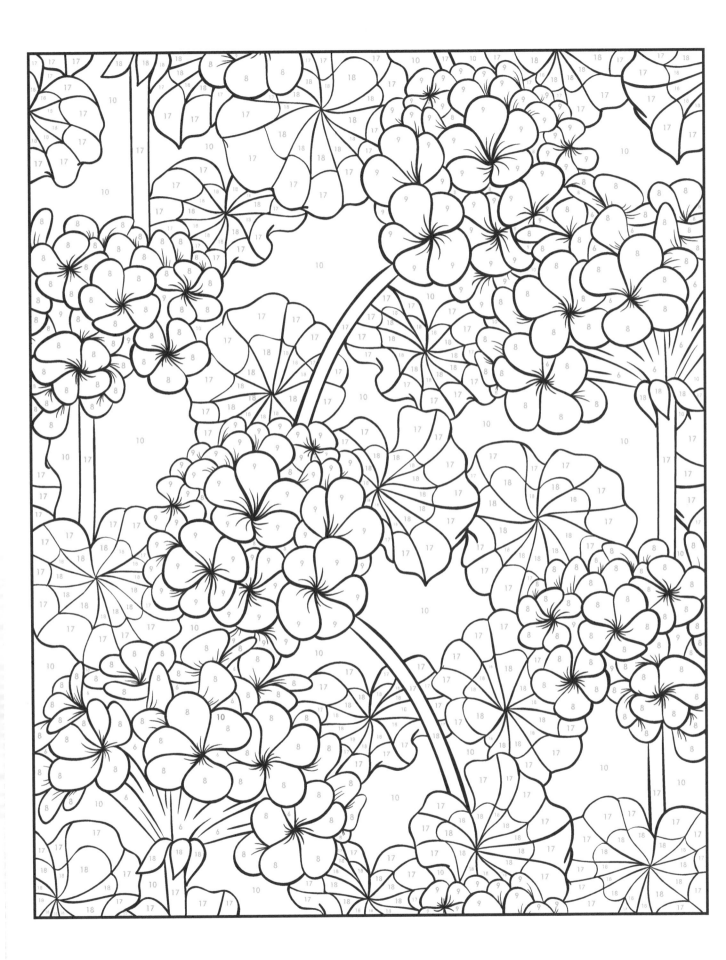

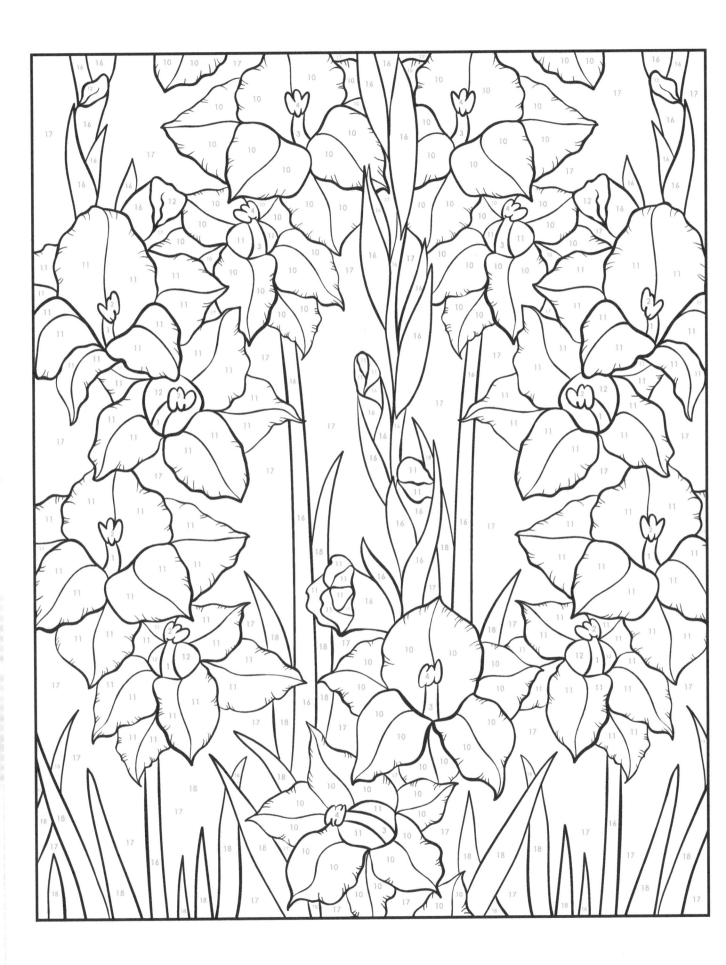

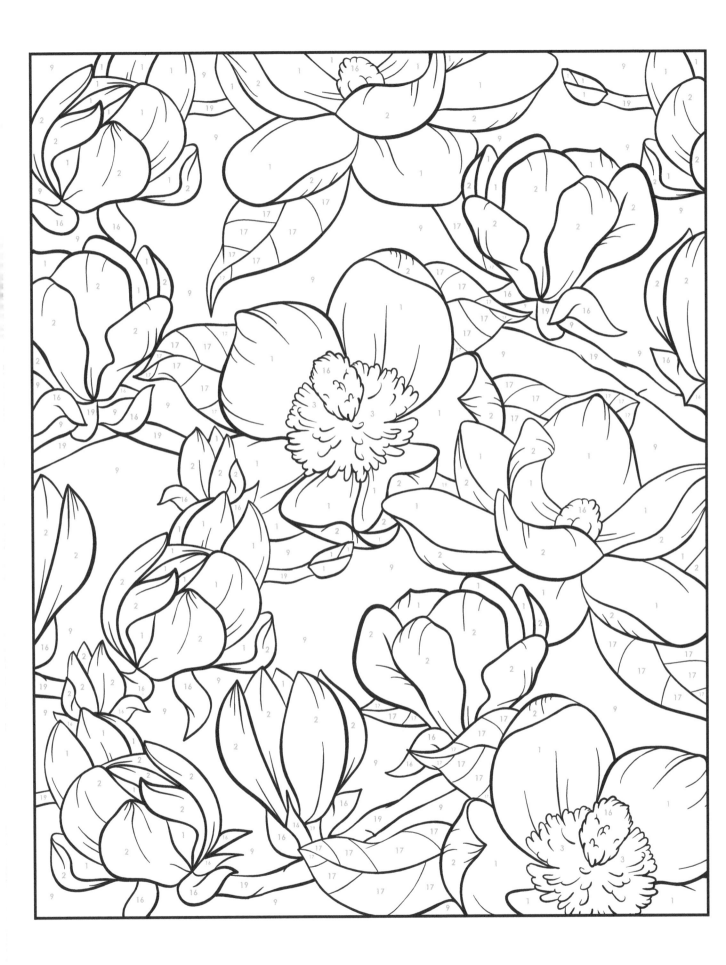

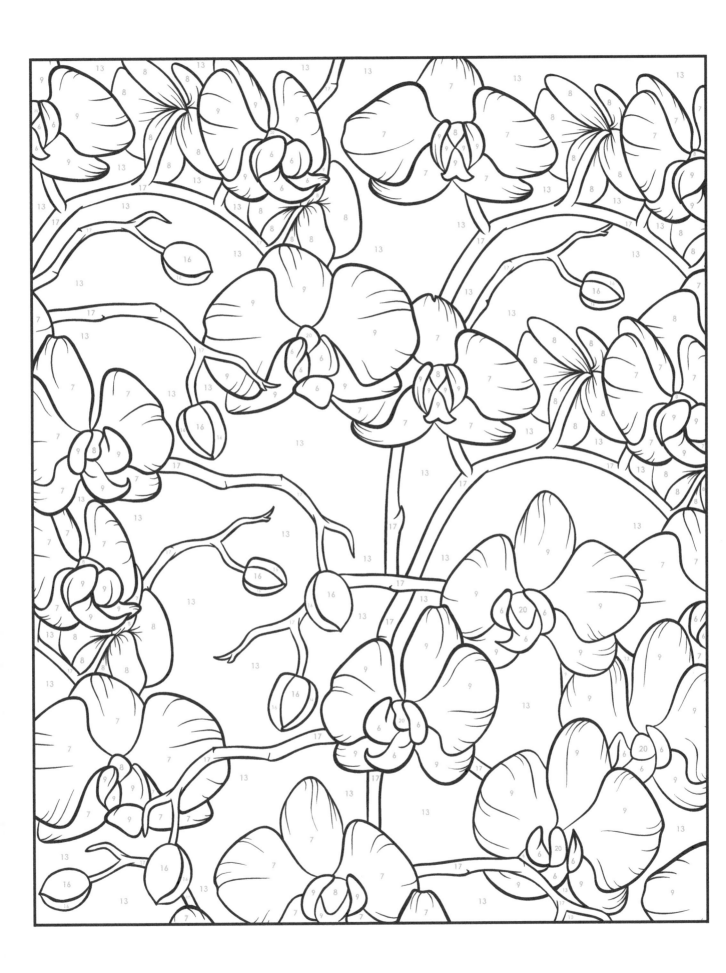

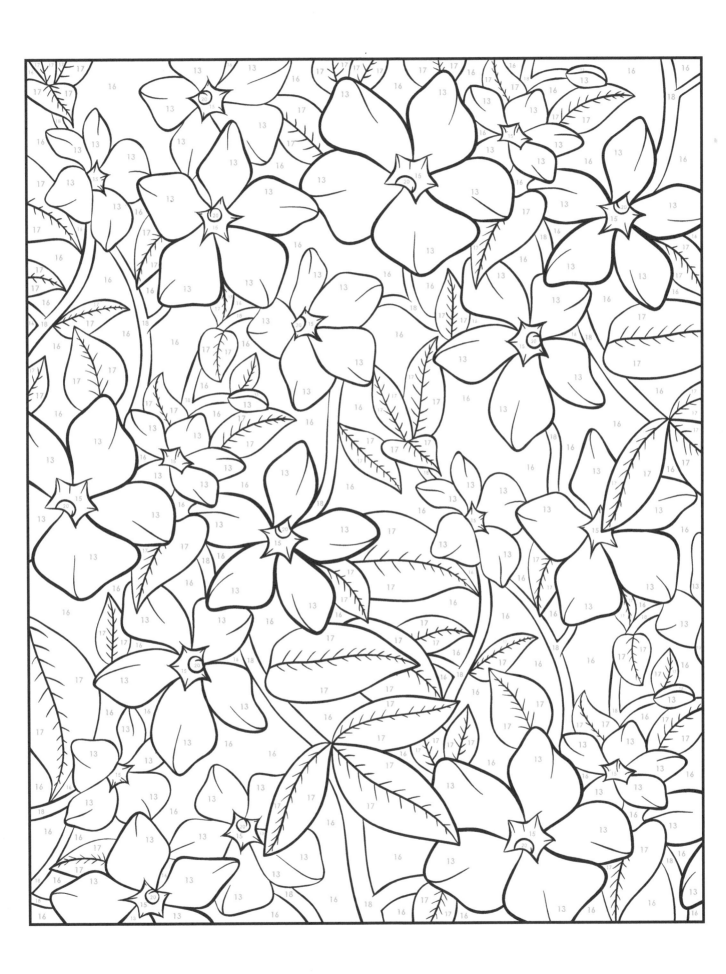

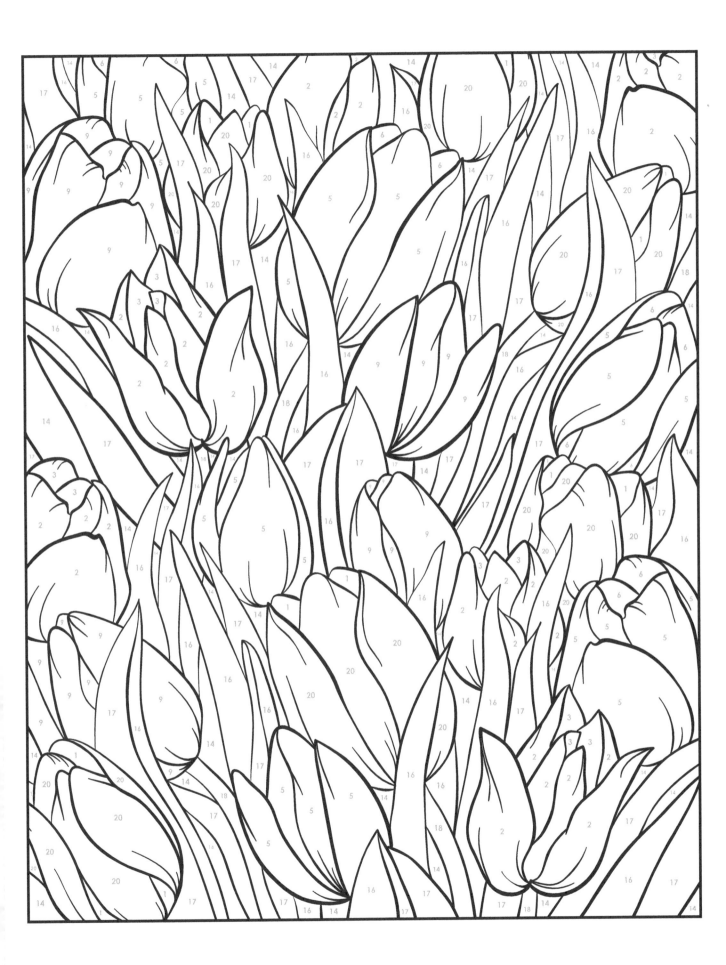